IN THE MIDDLE OF THE END, VOLUME II

AASTHA THAKKAR

To the ones whose elixirs are words,

This collection is for you.

Contents

Contents

Contents

Acknowledgements

First of all, I want to thank every co-author of this book for having faith in me as their compiler.
I'd like to take a moment to express my gratitude to everyone at Notion Press Publishing for helping me cross another box off my bucket list and for patiently answering all my questions.
And also to my laptop for not giving up on me. *inserts bread face*

Foreword

Sometimes, it's hard to see what the future holds
And most times, it feels like a steep climb, and that's alright
There's magic in details, the tender small gestures of love
And the way they all add up
When they ask why I can never explain
But a symphony played when you told me your name
And it sounded like a sign
Will you be my beginning, my middle, my end?
~ Song by Leah Nobel ~

Preface

Compiling the second edition of this book was even better, perhaps more superior. With the two volumes being published a year apart, one can notice the remarkable growth our writers have had. With more emotions, more pieces, and rigorous checks, we've given you our best. We have, of course, welcomed a few new writers to our family whose pieces are a refreshing garnish. Gather around, grab your snacks, the anthology is about to begin.

Aditi Gupta

Aditi's first piece was an adorable poem about her mother. In her most recent one, the character of the mother was killed. This is how she would like to describe her writing - raw, uncomfortably honest, and intriguing.

A mosaic of habits, likes, and dislikes borrowed from every person she's ever known, limiting her character study to just what she is currently obsessed with would be unfair. That said, we are still wondering when she would shut up about Mahabharat.

Making a new piece of media her personality trait is how she knows to carry on conversations. What is art if not inspired by something you love?

Striving to (occasionally) create something that you will not only love but also think about, Aditi has spent the last 19 years scribbling all kinds of words in her various diaries. She hopes to continue the same for a long, long time.

CHAPTER ONE

LITTLE SAMAIRA

Samaira always believed that the sun shined brightly every time a tragedy awaited her town. Her walk back home from school was simple – she would beg Papa for a rupee that morning while Maa neatly lined her hair in plaits. The house echoed with her favorite cartoon character's voice as Papa finally gave in to her request. She was handed her tiffin and water bottle. She did not have a lot of books to carry since the incident took place but she would pout at her mother's attempt to rest the bag on her shoulder and feign a grimace as she was bid goodbye. Remember the rupee she begged for? She is now standing on her toes at the local shop trying to reach the counter. The seller recognizes her doe-shaped black eyes peeping from the counter and places the fresh ice cream in her little hands exchanging a thank-you with his kind regular customer.

"How was school?"

"Not burnt today."

"God really is benevolent. What did you learn?"

"Shakespeare's play – Macbeth"

Their usual banter was often punctuated with the shopkeeper stealing glances at the sky in deep thought. Samaira was patient but lacked the intellect to understand why he would look at the clouds quizzingly as she would give objective educated answers to his probing. She was in a hurry to go back home today as little droplets of sweat appeared on her forehead and she could lick the ice cream

from her fingers. Without waiting for a reply, she said,
"I wonder if we would have to study so much if Macbeth did not regret what she did."
"What did she do?"
"Killed the king with a knife. Then the lady went mad and saw blood everywhere. Blood here, blood there, blood on my palm and blood on my face", said Samaira as she exaggerated her teacher's imitation of the Shakespeare protagonist.
He did not chuckle at this and instead replied with a condescending smirk, "Guilt does that to a person." "But why would they feel guilty if they already know it is wrong and still choose to do it?"
"They believe that they can tame their conscience later. People who are born without a conscience are lucky too. Those men would aim a gun at your heart as mercilessly as a hungry tiger who leaps at a deer and tears his skin away. Their thirst is only quenched at the sight of blood, unlike the lady your teacher taught you about."
"That would have saved me from reading so many pages!"
The shopkeeper's attempts to remind Samaira how unforgiving their world could be always proved futile as, for her, the only thing that mattered was to savour the last bit of the mango ice cream before Maa caught her loitering around. It was time for her to leave to continue on her path.
The walk back home was not laden with the scent of fresh roses and little Samaira admired nature. While crossing the bridge, she had a habit of pausing right at its middle to admire the stillness of the river; the sun shining directly above; birds singing their babies a lullaby in the nest, and bees buzzing around pollen. This was that one time during the day when Samaira was away from teachers lecturing her, the chit-chatter of her school friends, a sensation blaring from the television screen, or the neighbour's policing of his wife ringing in her bedroom. 'Tranquility' - was a new word she learned in the morning. She did not know how to spell it yet if she had to pick a serene moment to describe what it felt like, it

would be this.

Her aunt lived a few blocks away from her home and little Samaira was credited with being a wanderer. She chose to take a detour. Fortune favoured her as she met her aunt just before she was leaving to pick up her children from school. Samaira's cousins were younger and conveniently deemed irresponsible by her. She would usually babysit them and desire their company to feel the smartest among all. Her aunt knew how much she loved being loved. She quickly asked Samaira about the drawing competition she had participated in and without answering, the little girl started rummaging through her bag. Out came a medal with a ribbon around it in all its glory. The aunt wasted no time in squishing her intelligent nephew in her arms, her cheeks red with happiness and eyes wet with tears. Samaira did not expect this reaction. This pleasant surprise is why she looked forward to being hugged by everyone but Maa. She was smart enough to realize her potential but Maa would not appreciate it regardless. She knew what her reaction at home would be – "Of course, he came first and not you. He is talented." Expecting her to praise Samaira's achievements were similar to a domesticated parrot's expectation of being set free by the owner. Both suffer as their caretakers, under the guise of ownership, claim to know what is better for them. She wondered if God chose stone on purpose to carve out her mother's heart. Upon finding no immediate answer, she wrapped her arms around her aunt tightly, buried her head in her bosom, and muttered a prayer hoping to be met with a pair of eyes devoid of disappointment.

Aunt had instructed her to reach home immediately without taking any more detours. She promised to bring her favourite sweet dish tomorrow if things are alright and hurried to bring back her children from school before dispersal. Despite being given clear commands, little Samaira was a rule-breaker. The otherwise observant nephew couldn't make out why her aunt fidgeted a lot and kept stealing glances at the flyers. They were perhaps put up everywhere while she was at school. The adjacent lane reeked of incinerated papers, rotten eggs, and a new adventure. She firmly believed it was her last true calling today.

As she poked her inquisitive nose in that lane, she was taken aback by how distorted it looks. There was no roof to protect people from the blazing sun which is why, it seemed, no sign of life breathed there anymore. The sight resembled the colour palette of black and white from Papa's old film CD. If she held a piece of crumbled cement walls that laid on the ground, to her cousins, they would mistake it for clay. Her staggering feet carried her forward in dismay and astonishment. One of the houses in the lane looked like that one part of the school no one is allowed to visit now.

She recalls that godawful day and its dreadful details. The memory is so fresh in her mind that you would believe it happened yesterday. The sudden shut-your-ears noise from the speakers, flyers being thrust at teachers, moving out of classrooms in panic, children being thrown in the field and in a moment, what lied in front of all of them blew up. Tragedies are often associated with darkness but that day, the sun shined with so much rage as if it lit a matchstick among the terrible mortals to suffer. The blazing room where they enjoyed reciting poems and creating art did not take long to become a wasteland. The elders relied on the children's goldfish memory to move on.

Numbness follows grief and everything else is reduced to a cycle of events. New governments came and left; the seat of power occupied by someone new; vigilante groups found something new to be angry about and youth took to the streets to protest again. Primetime was engrossed in another appalling news story as fathers eventually gulped down a good hot meal and mothers started lighting lanterns during festivals. Years passed away and on a fine day, as one mother plaited her daughter's hair and the father lovingly bid her goodbye, similar rumours spread embracing the town in a deafening silence. They had attacked the neighbourhood the day before and announced their desire to repeat the past with candidness in those flyers.

How nice would it be if Samaira did not have to learn those extra pages? A world without pain is all little Samaira craved. Let God put an end to her troubles as swiftly as men slaughter nature. A world unknown to her tears, the lack of her mother's love, the sight of knowledge turning into ashes, jealousy among siblings, a place enveloped with wilted roses, the heartbreak of losing a friend, and the wrath of the thunder.

Maybe God isn't as benevolent as it seems for the scorching heat now hurt Samaira's eyes. Danger bellowed and little Samaira was not a good runner. Her back to the flames, she fell headfirst on the ruins scattered on the ground. The scream which eluded from her lips fell on deaf ears of the town sitting still, holding its breath, face hung low. What flowed out from her broken ribcage resembled Lady Macbeth's psychotic episode - blood here, blood there, blood on her palm, and blood on her face. A world without emotions does not get to choose how its numbness begins.

It simply lays in a pool of blood unable to breathe.

CHAPTER TWO

MAHABHARAT : A BLAH BLAH BLAH INTERPRETATION

I do not know how to begin this poem,
So I simply Google her name,
The tragic heroine of the Hindu epic,
Did she really sleep with 5 men?
Was she a virgin?
Was she beautiful?
We know all about her and feminity but here are some very
important facts you need to know about -
blah blah blah blah
An epic which consists of over 1 lakh shlokas,
2 lakh individual verse lines,
And 1.8 million words in total,
Screaming its ideals, values, and norms as you turn page by page by
page,
Centers it's climax around this lady's disrobing, harassment, cries,
screams, tears, curses, trauma, AND a miracle,
The miracle of being used as a plot device
to invoke sympathy, pity and rage against
the perpetrators -

the villains,
Oh, the heartless lustful vindictive villains
upon whose triumphant laughter,
the husbands decided to show them their valour years later but ...
respectfully,
So, off they go in the forests,
serve a king respectfully,
lead a respectful life,
Listened to the god's respectfully,
And get the lady harassed again respectfully.
Now, this is a part we often skip
for a maid being molested by a king
doesn't sit well with the grandeur of robes flying, flutes playing,
women sobbing and men laughing;
popular iconography often winces
at another boring servant being abused
at the hands of an all-time privileged cis - heterosexual macho
male.
So, they rush through the next few pages,
highlight her helplessness and get him killed
Then blame our oh-so-poor tragic heroine
for being so beautiful
that now come the sensible, compassionate, respectful villains to
fight their own blood.
She seeks blood, she seeks revenge
The only time she'll use her fists
is to wash her long hair with the fluid
that oozes out of her enemy's heart
for her vindication is to be quenched.
She's too pretty, she's arrogant
A shame and burden to be born out of flames,
Her blazing locks a testament to her burning passion.
A commodity to be done away with,
A protagonist who appears once,
Her voice raised only to echo her brother's, father's and husbands'.

I do not know how to end this poem
Till I keep seeing her in an innocent face on the daily's front page,
a sensation on the idiot box,
In you, in me, in us.
We know all about silence and happy endings but here's why you
need to know her name - and blah blah blah blah

CHAPTER THREE

AN SOS

She doesn't need your help,
for she can easily make your skin crawl,
a muddle of black, crimson and red spots,
writhing deep in the folds of your brain,
getting oh - so - comfortable,
leaving an invisible trail behind.
You despise every time a sigh feels a little different;
a hand on your neck choking your breath,
her tail - a noose for your spine,
a hiss echoes - the bane to your beats,
and the eyes?
a dim-lit room for your mother's demise.
The venom's red is a shade darker than yours,
it's all yours to call,
a present received as you gently kiss the nape,
the lips continuously elude a smile
and her tongue greedily licks off the tears
when you weep as the sun shines bright.
Your mother wanted to throw it away,
"It stole your heart from you!", she'd claim,
her hands tempted to break your ribcage,
where it lied safe.
But you despise every time anyone tries to unlock the prison,
so you tiptoe to her room, dim the lights,

let the fangs spread
and gently kiss the back of your dear mother's neck.

CHAPTER FOUR

PERHAPS, REALISM

I see him offering flowers to my mother's grave,
kindness clouding his eyes,
a mist of calmness surrounding him,
he smiles as I walk by and waves a familiar greeting;
I wake up.
I see him again,
with her,
they are both engaged in a similarly charged conversation,
hands are flying, the cutlery falls,
it clanks against the tile again and our eardrums shut down,
she looks eerily pretty today, it must be the red light,
do you see or does the fog blur your gaze?
Her lips curl up, we know what is coming,
he doesn't notice her hands at the platform,
he thinks it's a reconcile and wraps her in a warm embrace,
it is unabating and comforting, his arms at the small of her back,
little does he know, her fingertips are still teasing the blade ever so
slightly;
"yes, the wound is too deep to be tended to. I'm sorry for your
loss"
the doctor says, a rehearsed lullaby,
I wake up.
"Love has a dream-like quality to it"
my father reads,

she doesn't shyly meet his gaze this time,
we look where her thumb circles in motions,
his marks on her wrist,
a shred of evidence from the night before,
wasn't he wearing his favourite crimson shirt?
I cannot recall,
Can you?
did he reek of intoxicated foolishness too?
did he pin her down and didn't hear her pleas?
tell me, did it end like it always does?
I wake up.
I see him and her behind me,
they look back at me from the mirror,
through my eyes, you perceive them,
but they are me.

CHAPTER FIVE

IGNORANCE IS A BLISS

So, when you tell me about things
which illuminate the sky
And when you speak
fills the colours of your cheeks on a such a way
that it reaches the corner of your eyes
I ask you to stop.
Because, listen,
you have a knack for things which petrifies my soul,
hilarity escapes my throat as fetid facts slip down flippantly
and try to make space between memories;
memories which are so goddamn old
that I remember it as something I have
witnessed and not felt.
They remind me of the time,
when my IQ was asked
as I realised that grades don't count
the number of neurons in my brain.
How I understood
that we see constellations
only because human beings look for
closures in incomplete spaces.
Why the dictionary cannot define

'courage' as "acting inspite of fear"
instead of "not being afraid"
So, listen. Shut up.
Because my mind doesn't find it enthralling
when you explain why Cancer and Gemini
are arch-nemesis,
or how mercury retrograde affects your relationship.
Don't tell me
how they clapped for you
and your parents were proud
when you stood first in class.
Don't ask my brain to swallow that
a few billion years later,
The Big Crunch will cease our existence,
we will down into nothingness
and that is when
these thoughts, theories, concepts and memories;
the goddamn memories,
will elude your exult.
Because, my darling, shut up
for ignorance is bliss.

Theera

Being Theera means being so many things at once. An engineer, a mathematician, a video editor, a gamer. But what being Theera really means most is being a writer. Over the past year, I've gotten into web content writing and copy writing along with writing short stories, poems, and even songs. Songwriting is currently a huge part of what I write and I'm learning to play so I can maybe someday produce my songs. I write about love, heartbreak, sadness, sci-fi weirdness, and moving on.

CHAPTER SIX

ENGRAVING

The leaves on the trees are slowly turning green again. Spring was coming around again. I'm sitting behind a bush in the local park near where I grew up as a teen. The local park had undergone some changes over the years. Some things remained though. The lamps were modern, the bricks of the footpath, re-laid but the engraving on the tree beside the south gate of the park still peeked its head. Not today though. Today, now, those changes hadn't happened yet. This wasn't intended to be a nostalgic trip anyway. I check my watch and watch the needles slowly turn to midnight. I turn my gaze to the footpath. Any second now, he's going to come around. And I'll be here waiting. Always.

~

There's not much snow on the ground now. Spring was coming around again. I learnt in school yesterday about weather currents and air patterns. How they change the seasons in tandem with the Earth. It was quite fun, with the teacher even telling us the tales people used to tell each other about the seasons. Tales of supernatural occurrences that happened on solstices and equinoxes. I for one, never believed in such stuff, but always found them to be compelling stories. It's quite a coincidence too, that tonight is the first spring equinox of the millennium. Or did the teacher plan it out? I wouldn't be surprised if she did.
As I approached the park, I noticed it was very windy. Much more than other nights I've walked through here. The tree beside the

south gate still had the engraving on it. I looked at it every time I passed by but still didn't know what it meant.

RU BLF PLMD DSL DILGV GSRH BLF DLG WRV

Gibberish, right? Almost everyone I know of has seen it and tried to figure out what it means. But it wasn't much of a big deal and people never gave it a thought beyond an interested chuckle. The worn-down footpath had some remnants of snow, still. A sign of possible global warming? I read about it in a book in the library but when I asked my teachers about it, they shrugged it off as mere conspiracy.

~

Finally! He's here. I watch myself walk down the path leading to my home. I remembered walking down this path so many times, lost in my own head, wondering about the world and its possibilities. And now, I have to defend myself. Make sure that the timeline stays normal. I've had some thoughts about what can happen if the timeline gets messed up. Granted, my thoughts were based on a comic book featuring The Flash. But you never know, what separates fiction and science. Not of what I've seen in the future.

I try to recall every moment of that night. Every second. Every leaf. Every gust of wind. Every sound. I turn on the camouflage meter on my wrist gauntlet on my left arm. It hides me from vision but I'm still vulnerable to heat and cold. And it was being very windy and consequently, chilly. I follow myself, hiding in the bushes and slowly creeping along. And then I see it.

The shadow rushed at my younger self from behind. I ran into it tackling it as it fell to the ground. And I hold it in place, strangling it till it gives up, disappearing into a puff of smoke. I look up to see younger me, still strutting on, ignorant as ever. Good. He shouldn't know of the horrors of this day. Not yet.

~

The wind was making weird noises. Like struggling. Like a voice reaching for air. It was probably in my head anyway. Thinking about the supernatural tales my teacher talked about had my imaginative brain on the run, I guess. But hey, if there really was something about, why would anything come for me? I'm harmless. Oh, well. It's probably for the best I didn't look back anyway. The guy who was following me on the sides didn't see me notice him. He had looked away for a split second and I'd caught a glimpse of him. Normally, I'd have ran but something told me I was safer being my usual self.

School went on as usual. The late night had given me some ideas for some stories, so I doodled them on the last pages of my notebook during science revision class. Revision of topics for the others, not for me though. I was bored, so I doodled. And the teacher didn't mind. That day in history, we learnt of Caesar's conquests. I had thought Caesar was just a fictional character purely from Shakespeare's mind. And there he was, as real as real can be. I looked him up in the library during lunch break. And that's when I found out about the world of codes. Caesar used ciphers (which are basically secret messages with a key word) to communicate with his military. And then I picked up another book. This time, on ciphers and codes. Substitution codes. And my mind went ahead on a rampage, playing with the patterns.

That evening, I went through the park again, this time, earlier than usual. I noticed the man from last night, but he didn't see me yet. Guess I was earlier than he hoped I would be. The tree on the south gate had the engravings on it –

RU BLF PLMD DSL DILGV GSRH BLF DLG WRV

Wow. It was so simple all along. It was a reverse alphabet cipher. I noted the letters on my hand and went home, still following the footpath. I noticed the man had disappeared.

~

He's seen me. I don't know why but for some reason, the timeline's changing. How had anything changed? The only possibility would be if he noticed me last night. Maybe some detail I missed. No matter. I've got to ensure that my younger self's path doesn't vary too much on his way to become me. I check my smart web for when the park would be built and turn on my Krono-key. The park around me changes in front of my eyes and I get to the beginning. Back where it started.

~

When I got home, I wrote down the cipher and I wrote down the key.
Key:
ABCDEFGHIJKLMNOPQRSTUVWXYZ
ZYXWVUTSRQPONMLKJIHGFEDCBA
which deciphers the code to -
IF YOU KNOW WHO WROTE THIS YOU WILL NOT DIE
Huh. Interesting. But not enough. Supernatural? Immortality? Give me a break. But someone did write this. A real person. I will find out. Maybe it was that man. The one who followed my movement through the park. I'll ask him tonight.

~

It's a rainy day. I approach the tree near the south gate, finding the shadow standing there, waiting for me. I chuckle.
"Of course, you got here. I should have known."
The shadow simply shrugs and walks in sync with me to the tree. As we join into each other, I write on the tree, the cipher that would inspire my life's work. That would enable all that's happening. Even though the temporal problems I have in my future aren't solved, at least I'll be there. To try and prevent them as much as I can.

~

The man didn't show up to the park. I checked around the bushes where I noticed him first. There were still remnants of his existence, but not anymore. Disappointed, I turn to head back home when I notice it. I'm standing on the footpath, hoping that what I saw wasn't true, that it was all in my head. But then, how else would I explain it? Supernatural? I needed to get to the bottom of this. And as I exit the park, I leave my shadow there, standing watch under the tree which promises immortality.

~

TIGHT CORNERS

Sing me my stress right now,
I know how
The coils of the rope can tighten,
Making full stops.
Sing me confessions now
I'm whole, how
Could I resist temptations?
Could I please stop?
All my friends can keep on with their lives
And all they know is who I'm not now
All of the signs and all of the noise is
Controlled and hidden on the sidelines
Rocking me no, "No" back and forth, for, for,
For, for, fall
See away my whole life now
When the time's right to fall,
Don't fall in love.
See my way just spark and burn alive,
Confused, calm, and crazy in my bones,
So put your faith in tight corners

CHAPTER EIGHT

AT DEATH'S DOOR

As I lay back and closed my eyes,
One thought stayed behind.
All my life passed in a moment,
All my life with you;
And I've tried but I can't not see
How you defined my every breath,
My every eon to come.
If not for you, I'm just another soul,
You made more of this heart
Than Gods could know.
And now I reach for
That black dark knob
Lain on the door
To where Angels would roar.
I try not to look back, and
I find you in my eyes;
Only to realize that
Our love has no demise.
Would my world end with you?
Or would my soul stay with you?
I have no answer yet, and
I'll be on the other side
Of the veiled old door
With shades of night

And people of lore.
And when you come
On your last walk away,
Know that I'm here,
And I'm here to stay.

Arshia Arya

As a writer, I would like to describe myself as self-conscious. My writing is very flawed not only in terms of technicalities of English language but also in terms of thoughts. I like to write about things that people agree to but that cannot happen all the time. But I always want people to agree with me which makes me write things which I don't usually believe in. The first time I got to know about Ramayan's real ending, whatever i wrote in my write up came to my mind but I neither said it nor penned down. This piece let me express myself completely. I didn't care who would counter me, I went on to telling my truth and doing Sita justice. It made me come out of my little shell of self consciousness as a writer.

CHAPTER NINE

REPENT AND VENT

When Sita returns to the arms of the mother Earth, Lord Rama is left feeling helpless, and it is then when it hits him what all he has done to her. Something so irreparable, he thinks to himself;

"Sita, you are gone, and now I am left alone. Now I feel what you must have gone through when I abandoned you. Oh! This extreme sorrow in my heart is not ready to leave me. Why is it now that I am reminded of all my wrongdoings? My wife, my pregnant wife, how could I send you all alone in the forest?

When I saw my two sons, I saw your beautiful eyes. I have thought about those eyes every single day since I sent you into exile. They have turned out to be so righteous. Your beauty and intelligence are beyond compare, and I always knew that I did not deserve you. I was born into this world to teach every person to follow the path of Dharma. The sole reason for my birth became the reason for our end.

It was a curse to be born as an avatar of Vishnu. Now I am left questioning what the right thing was. What exactly was my dharma at the time? Was it to send you away? Or was it taking my beloved wife's side? Sita, you could have been so much happier if there had been someone else who broke the bow for you.

I have hurt the one person who was ready to give up anything for me. I hurt the love of my life and now she is gone. This is what a man like me deserves. You made me realise where I went wrong. For my kingdom, I will let you go. Was it really my dharma to do that? As a human, I have all the right to go wrong, but as a lord, how could I make such a horrible mistake.

Sita, you have always been honest and proved yourself fairly. I was not even in the position to demand a trial by fire, but I did, and I cannot be more apologetic about it. I could not get my head around the reality. People's views and words got to me. I wish I could say, "Mistakes happen. I am also a human. "But that is not true. Lord Vishnu reincarnated to this to show the value of being virtuous, but it just made me do the worst possible thing a "Pativrata" woman could go through.

Sita, do you remember when I used to go hunting and get you a bouquet of handpicked flowers? You used to get so delighted by these "small acts of love," as you would call it. When I received your token from Hanuman when he visited you in Lanka, all I could think about was the day I free you I will get you all those flowers. How I will never let you go through any more trouble ever again. Instead, I became the biggest trouble in your life.

Oh Lord Vishnu, I was supposed to be your avatar. I was supposed to take decisions with utmost truthfulness and morality. Do you see what I have done? Am I really an incarnation of the most strong deity? I have tested my wife's chastity, I have abandoned her even after she proved it and when I saw her again after years, and I demanded a trial again. You made me do it! You are behind my actions. The mother earth took Sita back into her womb and I am left her trying to apologize for my sins. Lords do not sin then how could I? I threw away the most wonderful time of my life and I probably deserved it. Sita, I take responsibility of injustice I instilled upon you. Till the end, you did not gave up on me, oh what I can do to have you back right now.

I guess all men, be it an avatar of Lord Vishnu or not, we trample your honesty and strength. We put you through hell and make you want to turn back into dust. I want all the men in this entire world who thinks that they are taking decisions on the basis of virtue, fall back into my avatar of Lord Vishnu and reanalyze your choices otherwise you will be left agonizing over your faults."

Anuja Tripathy

Hello! My name is Anuja Tripathy, and writing is my way of expressing myself.
I love it when people find my poems relatable or when my writings bring smiles to people's faces. It really motivates me to keep writing more. Times have been terrible, and it hasn't been easy for any of us, so I just hope that through my poems, people feel a little more hopeful and at least a little less anxious. Just like books, my poems have always been there for me, and I hope everyone likes what I have written! Happy reading!

CHAPTER TEN

WHY BE SO HARSH?

We all are in the middle of a pandemic,
And oh, how uncertain and messy everything is,
There is just so much of fear surrounding us,
Then don't you think its high time we talk about how our mental
state really is!
There might be some days which drain you out a lot,
Or maybe some experiences which make you feel lost,
Stop being so harsh on yourself,
Leave everything for another day to sort!
If you ever feel too overwhelmed with everything,
Not knowing how to process your thoughts,
Breathe in and out slowly my friend,
Because for too long you have been holding in a lot!
Life might seem to be going too fast some days,
Or maybe you might feel like you are stuck,
But my dear, how can you forget about all the progress that you
have made,
No matter what you have always made a great comeback!
I know you struggle to tick things off your 'to- do' list,
I know you are trying and giving your best,
I don't know if somebody has said this to you lately,
But I am just so proud of you for not giving up no matter how
scary at times it got!

For days when it gets difficult to take a leap,
Let's smile and take some baby steps,
You so easily give everyone else so many chances,
Then why not do the same for you and maybe for some moments,
heal and rest?
Don't ever feel dejected thinking it's just you who is struggling,
Because trust me you are not and never will be alone in this,
It might be pretty confusing to figure everything out right now,
So, for now stop being so harsh on yourself and I promise you we
will get through this!

CHAPTER ELEVEN

HARSH WORLD

Sometimes I wonder how this world can be so cruel,
How do some people so easily harm others?
How can they be so selfish and inhuman?
How can they even imagine hurting the soul of another?
Back when I was a little girl,
Whenever we would be walking through a lonely street
I remember holding on to my sister's hand tightly.
As she would ask me to walk faster and faster.
I used to wonder,
Why are we walking so fast?
What is this fear that is creeping inside us?
What was this sense of relief after reaching home at last?
As I grew up, I started understanding my sister's fear,
I slowly understood why we had to walk so fast those nights,
Why we always must avoid lonely streets,
And why we cannot feel safe anywhere and should always be ready
to fight...
So many news articles come daily about such crimes,
It sends a chill down our spines,
I was just 14 when our parents got us some pepper sprays,
I could see their fear as through their eyes it shined.
Even today when I have to open the door,
I first need to make sure my shorts are not too short,
Oh wait, I need to check if I need to get a dupatta,

Or it will be better if I go and change my attire completely as
the last resort...
I am pretty sure that I am not the only one who goes through all
this,
I am not the only one who gets anxious on lonely streets,
It's heart-breaking to see all of us live with such apprehensions,
Its heart-rending to see the world not becoming a better place for
us and oh its such a huge defeat!
We live in a world where a man can murder his wife in broad
daylight,
Where so many women suffer every single day,
Where speaking up against the wrong and unfair things makes us
angry feminazis,
We live in a world where people claim to believe in equal rights yet
refuse to call themselves feminists!
I find it funny how normalized all of this is,
How easily people judge us based on our choices,
How easily people comment on us and our appearances,
We burn in pain and hide our tears while the world simply enjoys.
I don't know if the world will change,
If people will understand us and our struggles,
But I choose to be hopeful for a better and safer tomorrow,
Till then, to feel okay, I will go to my mom for some much-needed
cuddles.

CHAPTER TWELVE

HAVE FAITH

To the one who is reading this,
I see you struggling every day,
I know how much you pray and wish for a better tomorrow,
I know how hard you try to make things work out in every possible
way.
I understand how hard this pandemic has been on all of us,
How overwhelming everything is right now,
But look at you still handling everything so well in midst of it all,
Look at you being so strong in such harsh times as now.
I know there might be days when you feel anxious,
Days in which you might feel powerless and worn out,
But know that you are doing all that you can,
By taking care of yourself and your family you are doing
everything that is possible and can be done.
If you are a sensitive soul,
Trust me I know how hard it is to see so many people suffering
outside,
All those news updates can be very draining,
So why not take some breaks from social media and for a while
leave everything aside?
I know we all are worried about our loved ones,
Never can we even imagine anything wrong happening to them,
And with this pandemic getting so severe,
I know it makes your heart heavy as you get scared and worry

about them.
Things seem pretty dark right now,
And I know it is tough to be positive and hopeful in such times,
But hope is all that we have with us right now,
So why not have faith that we will for sure overcome this tough
climb!

CHAPTER THIRTEEN

QUOTES

When it gets difficult to keep moving ahead,
It's okay to stop and take some moments of rest,
Because darling you are only human,
And all that matters is that you just keep trying your best.

Today before you go to sleep,
Give yourself a tight hug and a pat on your back,
Its high time you start celebrating your little victories and baby
steps,
Remember that you deserve all the love and there is absolutely
nothing that you lack!

You always have the nicest compliments for others,
You always see the good in everyone else,
But how much longer will it take for you to say you love you,
When will you be kinder to yourself like you are to everyone else?

Ananyaa Sharma

Yes, All my write-ups will be dark.
Users can proceed with caution.
Just a Gen Z writer who hasn't gone past the emo phase of their life.
My favorite quote: "Give up on your dreams and Die" ~ Levi Ackerman.

I Want To Light A Matchstick

I want to set fire to this relationship, I want to light that burning
matchstick.
The threats and screams have grown numb in my ears,
All the expected casualties have formed into plausible fears.
I am neither scared nor surprised that my personality is fooled and
ruined in shreds.
I want to set fire to my blazed nest.
Bruises, cuts, pain, love; bearing it all without a tear stain seen.
Blinded in love with a natural beast,
I have nothing left but this broken body,
The only matchstick left to be burnt,
I want to light this matchstick.
Consume my beloved,
Into my everlasting loveable flames,
Consuming everything in this nest, as a whole.

CHAPTER FIFTEEN

RESTRICTED FREEDOM

There is an invisible air. She desperately seems to gasp to breathe.
There is a cage in her freedom that dramatically creates her existence to an introvert.
There are tears and bookmarks in her book friends that shall never been seen.
A rising rage in her that cease to exist for childish reasons, the reasons that are important to her.
This poetry wasn't meant to be rhymed if that's what people like to see.
It's a poetry about a growing woman with limited boundaries.
Yet, she dreams to touch the immeasurable taste of friendship and joy, for that taste rarely makes it to reality.
The isolation from siblings and family, made words a super power and pen a weapon.
The for so ever dusted books, let out a proud and powerful chuckle.
For that's where her obsession and love of her oppressed expression began.
I don't want to exaggerate her limited freedom, but it's suffocating to see
What her peers are free to do and what the chains of conservative traditions , chain her from doing.

And this could go on and on for women in her household.
As anger burns them seeing the men of the same household,
walking in freedom.

45

CHAPTER SIXTEEN

DEVIL'S CHILD

And yet again
I stand in front of this forsaken grave.
Trying to assure myself the death of my reaper.
Yet his memories haunt me in the
back of my head.
My mind running all over that one day this devil will awake again.
For his offspring forcefully resides in my womb.
I poison myself and attain the sin and cry of happiness as his little
dead soul leaves my body for the good.

CHAPTER SEVENTEEN

AN ABANDONED TRIP

There is a hustle and bustle running in a warm house of a warm
city,
a dangerously unplanned trip and hovered over a hasty packing
and a family trip to love lost home.
Breath in this cool breeze once again my dear, for how long will it
stay always remains in fear.
Take pictures to capture the frozen memory for it soon just
become an un real aspect of future life, as Earth slowly crumbles
into a dark gobble place.
Post it up on your instagram that may slowly become "cringe" to
your future children, try and find comfort in this polluting
breathing.

CHAPTER EIGHTEEN

How I'd Sum Up the Year 2020

Stress and pressure has been engulfing my entire being,
a regular routine has turned into a nightmarish dream of a chaotic
quarantine,
irritation and anger itch into my skin and eat up my entire kin into
pieces,
a dark shroud surrounds the world as the mere ear buzz
transforms an entire nation into laughing stock meme.
Yet, people let themselves for ever so blindly let their corrupted
leaders, kill an entire friendly kin.
What once were just movie theories, transfigure and twist the
already twisted reality and blast into a pain staking burden for the
future to clean.

CHAPTER NINETEEN

EDUCATION SYSTEM IS FLAWED

Maybe the words I write could fill up my empty train of circling,
baseless thoughts,
they cook my brain as if it was being thrown into a pot.
The tired eyes wish for the loads to pile down and lessen into more
important lessons,
like how to pay taxes or try to love and embrace yourself.
Yet, all I learn is the history and masks that pierce my common
sense into ton of broken glasses.
I don't like being a pessimist, but the world I have grown to see
and live in has taught me nothing but,
How to live, even with the fear of death; that has never been feared
by my soul.

CHAPTER TWENTY

WHAT'S IT THAT YOU QUENCH?

I have the words to explain;
The aching of my lilac soul,
Yet my tongue and fingers can't seek;
Which would fit? One monolithic term.
Its so diverse in languages learnt and lost, culture learnt and
grown.
This body moved around severely; to suddenly stop.
"What's it that you quench?" I ask, in case of any insight
"My uniqueness" Again lost in an abyss of search.

A HISTORY

If histories could brew monsters and mysteries;
Then why can't it breach majestic queens
And homely Kings?
Queen waging wars shameful?
Rather it be dazzling to see strong breasts battling so fiercely.
Moving faster than the blink of an eye!
Taking everyone away in awe with her skills and scars.
Heart warming to imagine a King hold a toddler heartily,
Understanding subject's queries;
Handling the castle tenderly, yet disciplined and fearly.
Hold the barriers of love making dry and high!
Maybe, they're graves and history are yet to seem
Not dug deep.

Asish Alman Guru

Finding the best possibilities in this multiverse of infinite possible boxes of events. Hey! this is Asish Amlan Guru form XIM University. I started writing small thoughts and poems 2 years ago, and found it as the best path to express my frequencies and vibration into the aura of magic.

CHAPTER TWENTY-TWO

Thy Peace Is What Identified

Peace is a sound that is heard by not all.
Peace touches your skin, in the form of that early morning breeze.
Peace is a play that is played by every tree, with its leaves and
branches waving like a pentagon figure.
Peace is a moment where materials aren't involved.
Peace is where you find the light blue sky,
so much smooth,
so much bright,
but still sleeping with no much affairs of fright.
Ah! Can any of you imagine the pain of this peaceful sky, which
saw almost each and every destruction accompanied with its
sorrow.
This grey-haired charming sky, succumbed these all.... acting just
like a blanket to the eternity, covering the results of every thought
and its action.

CHAPTER TWENTY-THREE

HUE THAT FADES

Never try to be the iron rod which holds the multiple-coloured threads together, eventually there will be loss of dye on the threads and the holds will start wearing out to breakage.
Probably you will be the last one standing and waiting to rust ALL ALONE.
May be just like a sweet cotton candy stick, which was tasted by all, however its strength was bothered by none.

CHAPTER TWENTY-FOUR

BELONGS TO ALL

This may be yours, but that's mine...
Yap! Probably only the sky belongs to all
or maybe just because of its visible movement of clouds and stars
say so.
Is it the only reason, which gives the advantage to divide the land
between you and me? or us.

VERACITY

I don't know if I am correct or not, but
I find everyone around me so fake
Those laughs
Those anger
Those mood swings
Those split personalities
I find every other thing so much more fake.
You stand as my only hope, proving your reality every now and
then.
Please prove me the sanity of this world.
And drag me out of this duplicate make up copies, which is itself in
search of its original one.

CHAPTER TWENTY-SIX

B/W

Just look at those end lines, they are still a combination of black and white, where all dynamic colours are trying to touch each other's hand.
After a lot of twists and turns, changing those shades.
Those meeting points are known as Horizon, which is still standing as an illusion just like that of your own life.
Many come and many walk away with a new promise and some new fake rays of hope, but you still keep on walking with them to the edges.... even if the well-known out comes are just like the sky which never meets the earth and it's all again the black and the white.

CHAPTER TWENTY-SEVEN

EVASIVE OR UNCERTAIN?

Every diagram, every structure, every blood flow and every
tickling irritation going through the middle of the eyebrow,
running down through the head into the nerves of your spine are
just like a burning flame of thread rubbed with gun powder.
And you suddenly experience the strong burst of imagination,
picturing it all in the form of a flash of colours (mostly black, white
and green)
.... I see things changing, but they act like some prevaricate.
With a hush! I got up, I got up from the 4 AM dreams.
I don't know where I belong
I don't know where am I heading towards
"Pull over!" ... they said. They asked... "where to?"
I paused, I gazed. I said "where? ... what? I don't ...er!"
I was still on my bed, looking out the window,
the rising dark orange Sun, still too slow, but still moving.
My eyes moving towards the clock, which says half past 4.
Zenosyne may be? I jumped on the ground, stretched a little.
They kept their hand one my shoulder, and pulled a little,
And the voice asked, "where to?"
I answered with my other hand pointing towards the foggy roads.
[SIGH]
With big eyes, they asked again "what? You changed right?"

[Smiled]
Everyone did, when I waited and watched.
Now "we don't fall apart but...we're all supposed to".

Anwesa Nanda

Consultant by day, an overthinker by night. My life in a nutshell. Words are my oasis, my world rests within books, music, food, and interesting observations. "In the middle of the end, Vol. 1" was my first published work and I look forward to sharing my next set of thoughts through this one. You, my dear reader, hold the key to my soul in your hands!

CHAPTER TWENTY-EIGHT

THE RAINBOW

"No! Not on my terrace! "
"Yes Memsahib. She's there – three, too small, dark. "
"Can you take them away? "
"The mother won't allow anyone to come near them. Besides
I'm getting late. "
Audacity at her very best.
"Then do something to prevent them from moving. I don't want
them in my house."
Of all people on earth, why me? Yeah! Go ahead, try me.
I am terribly scared of cats. Phobia. And this foolish mother cat
had to start her crazy family on my terrace. On the top of it, Jatin
was having fun at my expense.
"Are you sure you're okay with my Delhi trip? ", he smirked. He
would be away – I have to handle the stray cats alone.
Bending over my dahlias, I replied "Are you going to cancel the
trip if I ask you to? No! you won't. But you want to earn some
brownie points. I can see through your plans Mr. Husband. "
"In that case, no use trying, eh? ", and he laughed like a zombie.
After driving Jatin to the airport, I came back home. Had to
complete the work at hand in a few hours and set on another
assignment. As I flopped on the couch, I heard sounds from the
pantry. I rushed in and saw that big fat mother cat. My kitchen was
in a mess. How the hell did she enter? Anger was replaced by fear
in a second. I shouted. Like I never had in years. Maybe she was as

frightened as me. She jumped off the counter - spilling all that was there. Almost in my direction and I yelled louder. She went past me, jumped out through the open window and everything was still again. I opened my eyes. Gone. I made sure I had sealed all doors and windows before sleeping that night. Maybe I should ask the maid to sleep in the hall tomorrow onwards. The thought was discarded in a jiffy.

I never ventured into the terrace though.

The next morning, I sent the maid to the terrace to check if the cats were still there. She reported back that the mother was not there. One kitten had died.

"Oh my God! How? "

"They die. Just like that. Maybe it was weak. "

Weak.

The more I thought about the "weak" kitten, the more I began empathizing with the mother cat. Maybe she wanted some food for her weak baby. I should not have scared her. I should not have ....

I sent milk for the other two kittens, again through the maid. I was less scared and more ashamed this time though.

In two days, one of the surviving kittens vanished. It was nowhere to be found. My maid told me that possibly, an eagle scooped it.

I did not know why the death of those cats caused such a tumult in my chest ... I knew the answer after a little bit of thinking though.

The mother almost abandoned the last of her kids. I never saw her after that mad encounter in my kitchen.

So, there was just one frail kitten on my terrace. I went up there. It was barely breathing. Smaller than a squirrel. Pity outscored fear. I gave it water and then milk. It looked full. It was walking – just like a toddler. I smiled and came back to the house.

I never liked the idea of pets. But this kitten! It needed help. A strange happiness enveloped me.

Jatin came back soon after. I told him about the kitten. He was kind of surprised.

"At least you'll get over your crazy fear", he said. This time I joined him too.

The next morning, I awoke before sunrise. Just as the sun rose, I went up – to the terrace. May be its sleeping, I thought. I came back home. Jatin and I came up a little later in the morning. It was still sleeping. Little did we know that it was gone. Ants had set their path through its skin.

"Why us? "I wept as Jatin tried to console me.

"No. It happens. All will be okay. "

He added, "Someday. Someday honey …. ".

That gave me hope.

Someday. Once again. For good. A tiny pair of feet. To grace our lives.

Author's note: Dedicated to all parents who are not blessed with children, yet. You, my friends, have created the legacy of love without the biological tag.

THE ABANDONED LETTER

Dear You,

Writing to you calms me. I love you for that. I love you otherwise too. Maybe I'll never be able to tell you how much I love you.

Everything is fine. Not the sort of fine when you were here but nevertheless.......fine. As usual, Emmy's dentist asked her to give up sugar candies. She's not going to give them up anyways. She asks for you. I guess she wants to consult you about it. My optician said that it was time I use glasses. Finally! Remember how I used to rue the fact that I didn't have glasses. You always said it was good. To look into my eyes directly. Ah! Those were the days.

I have not heard from you since long. Talk to me soon. Okay.... I'm inviting myself to your place. Emmy can stay with my mom, for a change.

With love,

Me.

P.S.: I'm posting this from the same mailbox where we first met. By Jove, that street has awful traffic. People get killed.

Author's note: My take on an epistolary love story. Dedicated to the almost forgotten art of letter writing.

CHAPTER THIRTY

NOTES ON HOW TO IDENTIFY OPPRESSED WOMEN

Oppressed women look lissom to the eyes of predators.
They have most perfect faces, par anyone's imagination.
They house fear in eyes, masking it generously with kohl.
Noses are held high, lest someone suspects.
Mouths are gagged. They never wail or seek help or even do things
that attracts (un)due attention.
Bodies are marked, ridiculed and trampled upon.
In the remotest corners of their hearts, they bury all dreams,
aspirations and desires.
They have lost hope, faith and soul.

CHAPTER THIRTY-ONE

PROMISE ME

Promise me not to wither away,
For you were once the object of my love.
I was smitten at first sight, but you never knew,
You were the one I yearned for secretly.
With familiarity, the magic spell broke,
I realized your vulnerability, your weaknesses.
I stepped back. Perhaps it was a sham.
You ceased to charm me.
With time, I started to loathe you.
Your presence annoyed me.
But when you said, "I wish I were dead",
Something tugged my heart. I froze with fear.
I don't exactly know what holds me unto you,
Is it affection or the thought of separation?
In love, maybe, you never loved back.
In hatred, I fancy you are around, hating me back.
Promise me not to wither away,
For I want to be the object of your hatred.
Author's note: When we need someone to hate or be hated. Maybe
we desire some darkness at times.

CHAPTER THIRTY-TWO

FORGOTTEN

15ᵗʰ May 2021. Mayank's thoughts on vacating their flat.
I found one of your pictures today.
Pressed in one of my old wallets.
Also a few pieces of paper,
I guess stained with your lip colour.
Had locked the stuff and kept it away.
I'm changing houses,
So, I had to check all cupboards.
Leaving them here. Forgotten.

1ˢᵗ June 2021. Monika's thoughts on discovering something at her new flat.
New house. To forget an old love.
Found an old wallet with pieces of paper.
Stained in lip colour.
Brilliant red. Must be forgotten.
Author's note: Love is everywhere, ain't it?

CHAPTER THIRTY-THREE

A WINDOW

I once wished my room had a window.
I could watch the world pass by.
Like bougainvillea flowers merrily drifting in the winds.
Fragrance of love wafting in the air.
The streetlamps glowing yellow.
Hawkers selling their goods.
The new mall flinging its neon lights unto the streets.
The crazy young crowds.
Random children chuckling as they walk.
Bike competitions.
The busy bees.
The old, abandoned and helpless.
The madman calling names.
The rains.
Gods visiting homes while playing with colours.
The police patrol.
The riots.
Someone could shatter my windowpanes.
So, I loathe windows.
Broken windows are painful.
Author's note: Where we live in darkness because the gaze of light
is scary

The Sikarwar's

Shital Sikarwar, Tanishka Sikarwar
This brilliant mother-daughter duo is set to warm your hearts with poetry, beautiful beyond words. Shital Sikarwar is in love with calm and soothing tunes; a human, with a heart, soul, and mind filled with love and passion for life. She's like a butterfly who is ready to leave her cocoon and spread her wings to fly.

On the other hand, we have Tanishka Sikarwar, with eyes gleaming with joy and having an inspirational zeal for life. Her heart which is as wild as the rose beats to the rhythm of the music and belongs to the dance floor. Football is her first love, and music is her solace. She loves challenging herself each passing day. She has finally started trusting the process and in the process loving herself.

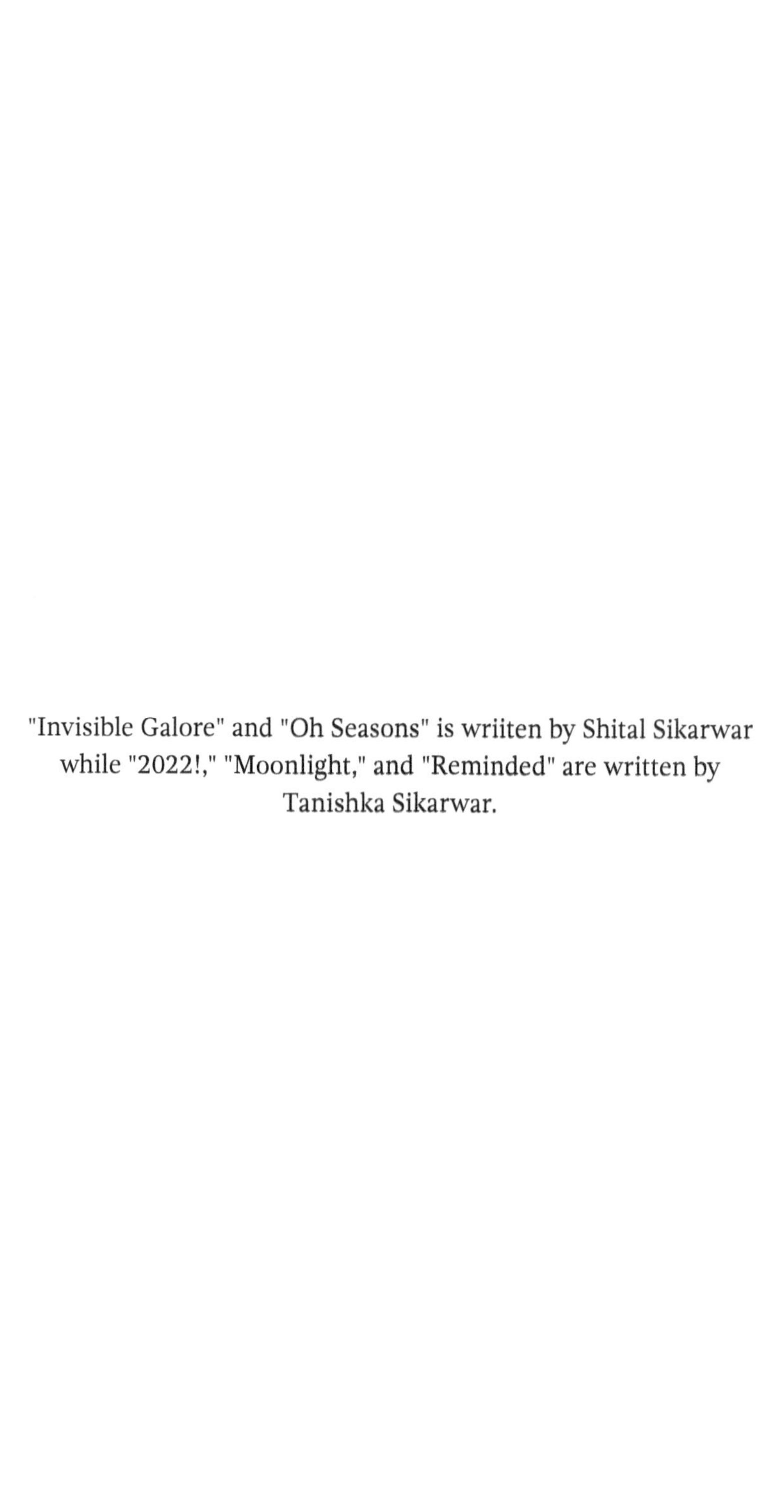

"Invisible Galore" and "Oh Seasons" is wriiten by Shital Sikarwar while "2022!," "Moonlight," and "Reminded" are written by Tanishka Sikarwar.

CHAPTER THIRTY-FOUR

INVISIBLE GALORE

The invisible strength to keep going on
Is like the string tied to the mortal kite flying up high
Where to when and how it will fall
is not on his mind
Through the winds gushing it hangs on even more carefree to
reach the top of the clouds and to feel light .
That's how it feels the joy and happiness of a wonderful flight .
The invisible voice deep within speaks words of wisdom to
keep fighting the dark horses deep inside
The words may be simple but are so heavy they applaud your
efforts making the echoes of pain vanish away
That's how you are awarded with the crown of being an hero
The invisible sound of silence sings out the rhymes and
rhythms which make you to sing along
The music created may be seen so electric sounding like the
gushing waves of the ocean bringing the tides to the shore
That's how you know you need to embrace yourself only then will
you have peace and achieve your goals .

CHAPTER THIRTY-FIVE

OH SEASONS

This longing to be loved the way I have never longed before
Waiting for the sparkle in your eyes
To help me see the spring flowers bloom outside
Longing to be loved and to love the way I love the spring that
brings splendour of the vibrant colours of the blooms giving me
the hope that seasons are changing and so will my times
Oh! Longing to be loved the way I have never longed before
Missing the warmth of your arms to help me feel the Sun ray's
on my face
Longing to be loved and to love the way I love the sun rising with
its orange warmth during the dawn of winter mornings giving me
the brightness of life
Oh! Longing to be .....
Yearning the touch of your moist lips on my rosy blushed
cheeks bringing in the joy of the first rain drops touching the soul
of the soil
Longing to be loved and to love the way I love the fragrance of the
drenched soul ending the hot summer days and nights giving me
the rush to survive .
Oh! Longing to be loved ....

CHAPTER THIRTY-SIX

2022!

Once again, a year comes to an end
A year where we did not really expect much
But turned out to be so much better than that
We kept ourselves first this time
Not thinking about what others would think
Not thinking about what others would say
We did what made us feel happy, what made us feel alive
2020 taught us so much
2021 was the time to implement
Amidst everything we learned how to stay connected to our
roots, "on the ground"
BTS finally reunited with Army after 2 long years
Some even "skipped to the good part"
People went from the Maldives to Dubai
Spider-Man finally made it to the theatres but had "no way home"
Sleeping during lectures does not feel that weird now as
cheating during exams is easy till now
Wearing masks is still a hassle for some
Another reminder to keep it above your nose to avoid any quarrel
Celebrations and weddings have changed to a hybrid mode
To follow the basic conduct of the code
It sure is getting better
Even if it is not visible
Let's not lose our hope

As we wish to come out from this battle looking dope
I wish we could say this was all a dream
But let's not become too extreme
I'm proud of you for coming this far
Let's continue together to reach that par
I don't know what's in store for '22
But I will pray for it to not be all blue
For we still have a long way to go
For we still have so much to do

MOONLIGHT

If only I could write a letter to you, I would
To thank you for being the only light in my darkest days
To thank you for staying up till 5AM just to listen to me
To thank you for not giving up on me
You are the one who have been through all the phases of mine
Seen me at my worst and even when I smiled
Listened to the stories that I could not tell anyone else
There is so many things to write about what you mean to me
But not the words who could do justice to the feeling
In you I find peace
In you I find happiness
In you I find beauty
And in you I find companionship
And now that I am going in my adulthood
I understand the feeling, the importance
You helped me love myself
You helped me stand up on my feet when I fell
You helped me through it all
And now, no matter what people say about us
No matter what they think about us
Even if they call me crazy for just talking to you
I will still continue to do so
Because Moon, you are looking beautiful
And I love you.

CHAPTER THIRTY-EIGHT

REMINDER

The reader has changed
And thus the story she reads
It is all too different now
What seemed easy is difficult now
What seemed possible has become impossible
The faith and the belief she had is now a joke to her
Love? You ask? No! that is just in movies now
Soulmate? You say? No! That is just a fantasy now
Everything has become a blur
For she had a lot to suffer
The pain fades away
But the memories still stuck in the back of the brain
She thinks twice before entering the place
For she does not want to be reminded of that face
For how long this will have to continue she asks
As she no longer wishes to wear the mask
There is no voice from behind her to assure that this will end soon
So she continues to walk the long path under the hot, bright sun
during the noon.

Dr. Uzma Jarullah

I am a gynecologist by profession..
Juggling between motherhood and hospital, never thought would
be able to pen down a word..
But then amidst all the trials Almighty throws at you, are hidden
opportunities..
Catch the subtle signs...just keep going!

ELUDE THE NOOSE

A turmoil that reigned
Spreading pain perceived;
Weary days fading into nights
Darker..longer than conceived.
"Forgive and forget ...move on"
Each concerned voice opined,
Sucked into the dark abyss
The advise stood undermined.
Wronged mutilated sentiments
Cast a shadow so dense,
No word, no light could penetrate
Notion of failure intense.
Stop, don't give up my dear...
The meek heart implored
You erred once alright, but..
The world remains unexplored.
Pardon yourself, NOT THEM
O Imperfect mortal, this once;
Trials pave for wisdom
Give life another chance.
As the realization struck deep
The knot slowly unraveled,
Surfaced a glimmer of hope
From the regrets unshackled.

CHAPTER FORTY

LIFE IS JUST A GAME

And I cried again...
Cried at the irony...
That I couldn't still decide,
What hurt more...
The fact that he could live without me,
Or that I was learning to do the same...
The pain that his betrayal still inflicted,
Or the acceptance that life is just a game...
The hurt of being looked at as inferior,
Or the fact that his achievements seemed lame...
And I cried again.

CHAPTER FORTY-ONE

THE OLD FOOLISH TENANT

One day I planned to clean,
Not my house nor my car
Something more vital...my life
Free of the pain and the scar...
Will dust it and mop it with
Focus, self-worth, and strength.
Paint it with a 'Hypocrisy' repellant
All across its full length.
Will finally put a sign board
That states loud and clear...
"Beware...The old foolish tenant
No longer resides here.'

CHAPTER FORTY-TWO

MY NEW SONG

Am trying to say no...
Stay away from my triggers...
Have been so long a yes-man,
Will be some days till it figures.
Each day is a step closer
To the point where I evolve...
Just need to shut all out
Who tend to break my resolve.
The actions seem not proper
My right qualifies as their wrong...
But am confident 'my own'
Will dance to my new song.

CHAPTER FORTY-THREE

A MOTHER'S PRAYER

World of dreams and frolic
Friends varied and infinite
Excelled on her borrowed notes
But didn't hesitate to backbite,
As she clapped on, without any bother
A concerned chide piped her mother.

Mind that gentle heart, my darling
It will beat longer...

Came the knight in armor
The Land of roses, Behold!
Witty words copper coins
Exchanged for her gold
Seeing her lost inside her own castle
Came the concerned whisper

Mind that gentle heart, my darling
It will beat longer...

Enacting the roles so vast
Amidst friends and foes

Silent tears, lonely nights
Recovering from the blows
Realizing her refusal to give up,
Came the silent prayer

Mind her gentle heart,
Oh lord, It will beat longer...

CHAPTER FORTY-FOUR

SUR AUR SAAZ

Sulajti zindagi, phir uske dastak se uljhi hai,
Kyu aaj apni woh zindagi si lag rahi hai?
Din kat jaate hai farz rishto ke nibhane mai,
Aur raatein tanhai ke aasu chupane mai...
Kayi lamhe beet jaatein hai iss intezaar mai,
Ki do pal bita lete hai woh hamare pyaar mai...
Nazm ek, fark kitna hai sur aur saaz mai,
Kaash do kadam chal lete woh hamare andaaz mai,
Kyu aaj apni woh zindagi si lag rahi hai?

CHAPTER FORTY-FIVE

DIYE

Yu ulajh gaye woh,
Hamare gharonde ki chamak me...
Ki hamari udassi ko
Nashukri samajh baithe.
Kaun batayein kitni shiddhat se
Jalaein the humne ye diye
Tanhai ke andhero ko
Mitaane ke liye.

Neha Ved WordPreneur®

Neha Ved WordPreneur® is a multiple-award winning Content Strategist, Media Consultant and Brand Storyteller. She's the Founder and Chief Content Strategist of PenVmedia®, a creative content studio built on the premise 'Content is the Hero that propagates your Brand Story'. The studio offers a bouquet of strategic content, branding and promotion services.

Armed with over 17 years of experience in writing, editing, strategy and media communications, she has worked closely with some of the leading media and publishing houses, top brands and CEOs to create content that boosts personal and company branding. She also offers editorial consulting and editing services for manuscripts, mentoring industry leaders and aspirants, both.

As an editor, Neha has edited a host of books, including autobiographies, self-help, personal transformation, fiction, 4 of which are bestsellers. She is a published author and poet, with her with short stories being published in 11 Anthologies, of which 8 are World Record holders. Neha is also on the Leadership team of brands, PR and Social media agencies and education consulting institutions, as their Communication & Content Strategy Consultant. As the National Vice President for WICCI (Women's Indian Chamber of Commerce & Industry) National Council for Reproductive Health and Rights, she strives to create a positive impact on women at large.

CHAPTER FORTY-SIX

WIND ON A DUST COVERED ANTIQUE MIRROR

Time... the all-powerful, the all-healing, they call it.
But time can be harsh; it can take its toll on anything.
And then one day... something which was once beautiful, is
now called an antique.
This mirror too was antique, more than five centuries old, the
experts said.

***

People told tales of the time when this mirror was made, and its
maker. He was the best carpenter in the countryside, hired by the
landlord to craft it for his son's betrothed. Being the only heir to
his father's abundant wealth and estate, the besotted fellow had all
the means at his dispense to woo his lady love.

She was a peasant's daughter, but her simplicity did not deter
him from in love with her. In fact, it was her simplicity that won
his heart.

His father was only too happy to comply with his son's wishes.
The girl's father had no dowry to give for his only daughter. And
so, not wanting to lose out on such a fine match for his darling, he
had agreed to become the landlord's stableman for life, as well as to

part away with his small plot of land.

It all worked out very well, for the landlord at least, for was on a land acquisition spree. And that plot was the most coveted piece in his scheme of things. Under the garb of facilitating his son's alliance, he had paved the way for his own dream to come true – a golf club for the elite.

The son was happy, the father was happy, the peasant was happy... but was the bride-to-be happy? Alas no! She was in love with the widowed milkmaid's son. But could he even hold a candle to the wealthy landlord's son?

It was thus, that the arrangements were made, the wedding was fixed, the date was set, and the price and prize were exchanged.

The mirror stood witness as the fathers shook hands. That night it gleamed. Its ornate artistry was to be talked of even weeks after the weeding was over. Chestnut brown in color, with scented sandalwood used strategically in the frame, it was highlighted with ivory and dark ebony. The knobs were made of pearl and Persian glass was embedded at the center. This mirror was nothing like anything anyone had seen before. It was a piece of pride especially crafted for the new bride, making her one of the most envied brides there had ever been, across faraway lands.

That night she stood in her matrimonial room, waiting to begin anew... memories of a lover etched in her heart and vows made to her husband committed to her mind. Her fingers gently traced the outline of her bridal gift. She looked at her reflection adorned in all that finery. The delicate veil of her bridal gown, that tiara perfectly positioned on her head, and her newest possession – her wedding ring. She was the befitting sight of new hope and lineage for her new family. But only the mirror reflected her blank eyes, only the mirror showed her, that what the world couldn't see - her real self.

He came in as gently as he could, but yet when he breathed near her neck, he startled her; may have even terrified her. To her, he felt like a ghost who had crept up unannounced from behind her. She saw his reflection behind hers and the look in his eyes told her what she must do. And so, she turned around and surrendered to his gentle, but firm and hungry advances.

Three months went by in a silent manner. Just when it appeared that the fourth too maybe pass by in a similar fashion, the "event" occurred.

For the past few months, the mirror had been witnessing it all - her blank eyes, her elegant dress, and the lack of her enthusiasm as she dressed for her husband who was returning from his quarterly tour of the estate; the rehearsal of her reactions to his dim wit jokes, her false smile and her attempt to show love in her eyes; a tear welling up as she finished preparing for her act, against her heart's desire.

But the mirror had also witnessed another side to her, the one that made her heart come alive. It has seen her being playful with her hair, looking at herself with a sense of pride for her flushed cheeks, and him running his fingers over her bare shoulders as she slid them to tingle her blossom; her coyness with which she hid on his chest, the intensity with which she dug her nails in his back and the passion of her climax on the same matrimonial bed; the love she felt for the only man she had ever loved - the milkmaid's son.

But even the mirror did not expect what it saw that fateful day.

Her husband came home earlier than expected. He was anticipating his homely wife to be taking her afternoon nap. He quietly slid into their bed-chamber, carrying a bunch of her favorite white daffodils, so that he doesn't disturb her peace.

And then it happened.

He saw his wife was asleep... asleep in the arms of a man he had never known or seen. In a flash, he picked up the stone vase lying nearby and smashed it on the man's head. The noise of the impact followed by the sound of his skull cracking up was enough to wake her up to a blood-smeared face. Her husband pulled her out of the bed and look at her consumed with wrath. As he saw her naked form, he could only think of the times he had tenderly caressed her, giving her all his love.

With revenge and rage battling inside of him, and love swelling in his heart once again, he gripped her by her hair. Frozen with grief and shock, she was a lifeless puppet in his hands. Rubbing his blood-covered hands on her shoulders, he roughly sat her down against the mirror. He rode her as violently as he could, channelizing his potent mix of fatal emotions.

With every thrust of his, the mirror behind cracked slightly. Chards broke and entered the back of her head, deeper and deeper, matching their penetration with his. At the moment that he had his release, he gripped her throat hard, ensuring that she remained still forever.

An hour he sat there, grieving over his dead wife... the only woman he had ever loved and the one he had murdered.

His father found him shortly, hugging his wife's blood-soaked corpse. He quickly summoned his trusted servants and had the mess cleared, the bodies buried, and the mirror's glass repaired. Rumors we spread about the peasant's daughter eloping with the milkmaid's son, leaving a heartbroken landlord's son behind.

Soon the bereaved husband began to complain of the mirror being a horrifying appendage in his room. He said his wife stared back from it every time he turned towards it. One day, unable to take it anymore he barged his head into it, attempting to shatter the mirage staring at him. His skull cracked and the chards entered deep into his head. It was poetic justice as if the two lovers had come together to avenge their deaths and destroy the destroyer of their love.

The landlord declared the mirror cursed and had the glass replaced. But soon the servants began to speak of silhouettes in the glass. The mirror was given off to the local furniture store. They say, since then, no bride has lived to see the morning of her wedding night, if presented with this mirror.

The myth spread so far and wide that the mirror was relegated to the attic of the furniture store.

Today, 500 years later, when the attic was being cleaned, it was brought out.

A wind blew off the dust collected on the old antique mirror...
was a new story to unfold yet again?

97

Shaikh Ramsha Kausar

An Astrophile with a wanderlust soul.
Channelizing my attribute of overthinking into something better
and trying to be less sarcastic.
I aspire to be nurturing spirit, a type of person whose presence
feels like light. A person who you can always count on and confide
in.
In love with literature, lights and flights and
A strong believer in Geet's dialogue "Jo kuch insaan real mein
chahta hai, actual mein, usse wahi milta hai..."

CHAPTER FORTY-SEVEN

LIGHT AT THE END OF THE TUNNEL

Sitting in a corner of my house
I'm waiting for you..
I'm missing you like a wolf howls
Tears in my eyes
Hope in my heart
One day you'll surely come and catch me while I'll be falling apart
you'll hold my hand , they'll call me by your name
You'll kiss my forehead and wrap your arms around me...
I'm missing you tonight a little more than ever
I don't know when will the day comes I'll kiss you forever.

CHAPTER FORTY-EIGHT

PEACE IN PIECES

The anger arose inside me
Making me go insane
No matter how hard I try to hide
The facial expressions know it's game.
I don't know if I'm wrong or others are right
The answer to this question is out of my might
people and emotions are wierd things
they change like seasons without giving reasons
And when they give
without counting their one they give yours five.
Everybody wants to be the king
Nobody wants to be the pawn
Forgetting after the night
Comes the beautiful dawn.
I don't know what am I
A person or a lone dead guy
The question that makes me hazy
Am I or the others crazy!
What is life and what am I doing
Is there any proof of my being?
Want to yell, cry and beat
O for God's sake turn off this heat
But tell me what should I do?
Question myself or become quite

Or rather run away
Till I'm out of the sight

CHAPTER FORTY-NINE

LOVING YOU FROM AFAR

I need a companion
But I'm trapped in this unrequited love
Because there's nothing I can do
Other than waiting for you
Maybe you'll come someday
Seeking me trying to find a way.....
I'm weak
Yet I won't show the sign of desperation
Don't want to feel that hesitation...
Hoping you'll show some sign
Coming out of your nutshell saying you are mine
It's okay if my imagination goes in vain
I'll live to have a glimpse of you from my windowpane...

Isn't It Crazy?

Isn't it crazy?
How we get attached to people that we know would never be with
us because we don't share the same destiny.
But our heart fell
Knowing the truth very well,
Making us sin
As we are the puppet of our own feeling,
No matter what the brain tells
We are Captivated under the love spells.
We dream even though we know we'll be crestfallen
As we live in our mundane world
Trying to make peace with reality
Imagining scenarios losing our sanity.

CHAPTER FIFTY-ONE

CRESTFALLEN

Under the moonlight I miss you every night
Wondering if you would ever be coming
around.
My heart longs and my soul aches just by remembering you
My day turn into nights and nights turn into days, praying and
hoping to see your face.
In flame of remembrance I burn
Wishing someday you would turn
But I was wrong all along
O heart this is not the first time you are wrong!
May be you'll learn not to build castles in air
Because each time it leaves you in despair.

Aastha Thakkar

Hello there, it's me, Aastha Thakkar!
I'm the girl whose in love with poetry, rain, books, and food. You can call me momo. A selenophile, I can daydream for hours on the end. The world is so crazy and brilliant that it leaves me speechless and I end up saying 'meow' when I don't have a reply to a question. I always have a book with me, wherever I go (You never know when you need it!). Professionally, I am an independent writer, a creative writing coach, and a mythologist. I can speak about Mahabharat and K-Entertainment for hours at end!
I've been writing for the past 6 years and this volume is the third title under my name. I hope you get to read many more of mine!

CHAPTER FIFTY-TWO

SINFUL REMINDERS

There are tears in my eyes that refuse to cry,
A book lying on my table with its pages dry.
There's a weird, strong urge in me.
To message you, to ask about you.
Where have you been,
What you have been doing.
As I bury myself in the words of this unaccustomed earth,
I can't help but think of you.
Every sentence, every comma, every full stop,
Reminding me of you.
Reminding me of the days we spent together,
Reminding me of your sweet smile in your picture.
Reminding me of the times when you asked about me,
Reminding me of the times when you held my hand helping me
cross the road.
Reminding me of the times we pressed our bodies together,
Reminding me of the time we spoke till you board your flight.
Reminding me of the times I reminisced about you.
Reminding me of the time we held each other for the last time,
Waving our half-hearted goodbye.

BLACK SWAN

Maybe you were my black swan.
Perhaps my white.
You were a perfect curse in disguise.
The perfect mistake I wanted to make.
The perfect smile I wanted to fall for.
Oh, what a crazy month it has been,
What a crazy year it has been.
What a crazy decade it has been.
For I cannot stop thinking about you
From the moment I first heard about you.
I was wondering how you'd look,
How you'd behave.
And to my surprise, you behaved the way I'd exactly thought.
The eyes filled with excitement,
And a smile pressed with wisdom.
A tongue which seldomly spoke.
A hand that helped me get back up after I fell in a mud pit.
A warm heart with a cold exterior,
A long face fits perfectly with your body.
We waved goodbye
And for ten times, Indra blinked his eye.
After a decade of longing,
I finally had a chance to meet you
But I just couldn't muster the courage to say hi.

Perhaps I was ashamed of how you perceived me,
Perhaps I was scared of how maybe you'd not like me.
For I spent more than half of my life engraving your name on my
pillow.
You cross my mind for more than just a fraction of a second.
You stay with me when I study,
You stay with me when I read,
You stay with me when I work,
You stay with me when I write.
You stay with me in every part of my body
Even if you haven't touched it once.
Perhaps, I don't even know if you think of me sometimes, maybe.
Maybe for a fraction of a second.
What kind of connection is this?
Despite knowing each other for a decade,
We can't even come close to one facade.

CHAPTER FIFTY-FOUR

MAYBE

The tears in my eyes are finally shedding.
After pages of scribbling.
I can't get myself to let go even a bit of you.
It's just been a second since I last thought of you.
And you're back in my mind.
I don't know if you'd be the same boy I met in my girlhood.
The same boy roaming around the resort in his favorite hood.
Did you grow up to be a man which I might despise?
Did you grow up to be a man I'll fall head over heels with again?
Maybe I'll text you tonight.
Maybe I'll send in an email tomorrow.
Maybe I'll look you up again on social media the day after
tomorrow.
Maybe I'll think about you again next week.
Maybe.
Maybe.
Maybe I'll pray for us to meet again.
Maybe I'll wish that we get a chance to say hi again.
Maybe I'll write about you till I have nothing more in my heart, my
brain, my body about you.
Maybe I want to meet you again
Maybe I never want to see your face
Maybe I'll never grow over my tiny infatuation.
Maybe it's not tiny.

Maybe it's not just an infatuation.
You linger continuously in my thoughts, in my words.
Will you leave me anytime soon?
Or will you come back to me the next second?

113

CHAPTER FIFTY-FIVE

DANCING BY YOUR SIDE

Wandering in the darkness
Around the pale moonlight
In the forest of the half dead
Fighting my fears and demons.
Every time I strike a blow,
All I think of is you.
The smile on your lips
And your hair falls like a cascade.
Our cherry flavored conversations,
And our moments in a darkened room.
I grab your hand under the sun,
Running towards the door of freedom.
Fluttering my eyes against the freshly risen sun,
I wake up to your faint footsteps dancing to the tunes of
Serendipity.
I woke up just in time,
Now I'm dancing by your side.
"I never kept you in secret, my love,
I just kept you to me."

And, that's a wrap for our second collection. I hope you enjoyed it,
in case of any doubts, queries, or suggestions, please feel free to
mail me, at aasthathakkar2612@gmail.com .
We'll soon see you with our third collection!
Please mail the above email address if you wish to be a part of
the third volume! Waiting to welcome you in our family!

Before you go, here are the Insta IDs of all the co-authors!
1. Anuja Tripathy - @anujaaaa23
2. Theera - @theeraology
3. Tanishka Sikarwar - @tanishka_20
4. Shital Sikarwar - @shitalsikarwar
5. Shaikh Ramsha kausar- @ramshashaikh21
6. Anwesa Nanda - @clauses_and_pauses
7. Dr Uzma Jarullah - @teleportedme
8. Ananyaa Sharma - @writer._from_the_shadows._
9. Neha Ved - @nehavedwordpreneur
10. Arshia Arya - @__arshia___
11. Asish Alman Guru - @asishguru
12. Aditi Gupta - @adxtigupta
13. Aastha Thakkar - @throughblackandwhite_